JUST AS BLUE

Andy Croft

FLAMBARD

ACKNOWLEDGEMENTS

Versions of some of these poems have previously appeared
in the following publications: *The Coffee House,
London Magazine, London Voices Broadsheet 37,
Other Poetry, Penniless Press, Pitch, Poetry Review,
Prop, Scratch, Subtext, Terrible Work* and *Thumbscrew*; 'Replay'
was broadcast on BBC Radio Four on the morning
of the 1998 League Cup Final; 'Letter to Randall Swingler' was
first published in 1999 as a pamphlet by Shoestring Press.

The following poems carry specific dedications:
'Grisedale' is for Jean and Geoff Croft, 'Digging for Victory'
for John Lucas, 'Letter to Randall Swingler' for Judy and
Edward Williams, 'The Mask of Freedom' for Stanley Forman,
'Marxism and Smoking' for Pete Challoner, 'Song' for Tim
Dalling, 'Crash! Bang! Wallop!' for Adrian Mitchell, 'The
House Beautiful' for Peter Salt and Liz Lush, and 'Santa
Espina' for Dave Goodman.

First published in England in 2001 by Flambard Press
Stable Cottage, East Fourstones, Hexham NE47 5DX
Typeset by Barbara Sumner
Front cover photograph by Dermot Blackburn
Cover design by Gainford Design Associates
Printed in England by Cromwell Press, Trowbridge, Wiltshire

A CIP catalogue record for this book
is available from the British Library.

ISBN 1 873226 44 6

Flambard Press wishes to thank Northern Arts
for its financial support.

northern
arts

Website: www.flambardpress.co.uk

CONTENTS

... the first verdict seemed the worst verdict
When Adam and Eve were expelled from Eden;
Yet when the bitter gates clanged to
The sky beyond was just as blue.

                        (Louis MacNeice)

They say Havana Cuba
Is the place where I should go,
But what's on my mind
No-one will ever know.

                        (T-Bone Walker)

Stay quiet, and exercise what love you may
To infiltrate the stirring soil, or knit
The roots of some few grasses. Do not look
For anything but anger from the sky.

                        (Randall Swingler)

GRISEDALE

From Stony Rigg the swollen hills
   Rise up through mist and sodden moors
In a tidal wave of rain that drowns
   The dale below as flooded gills
Leap into Grisedale Beck, then down
   To Garside Head, the road to Hawes,
To pour itself into the Clough,
   The Lune, the sea, which cannot drain
This mountain dry of Pennine rain,
   As if the seas weren't full enough.

The radio brings news from Asia,
   A long way from this cold and wet.
Where sabre-toothed economies
   In Thailand, South Korea, Malaysia
Now eat their tails and Japanese
   Investment banks collapse in debt,
As the Yen and Won come crashing down
   Like trees that fall into the river,
And now we all must face this weather
   Like sheep in roofless, dry-stone barns.

There's nowhere safe from the irrational
   Workings of the markets; seas
Of greed and graft devour the earth,
   The rain of money's international,
And bursting banks are never full enough.
   Outside, the mist begins to freeze.
This rain looks set to last for ever.
   We watch it wash away the light,
The fire grins; we're warm tonight
   But who can now predict the weather?

A long way from the Pacific Rim
    The cold is crying through the lock.
Outside the ranks of dripping fir
    On wooded hillsides add their grim
And lonely beauty to the blur
    Of green and grey. Inside, the clock
Slows down like rain through dripping trees.
    We pour ourselves another drink
And stare into the fire and think
    Of sinking hills and rising seas.

DIGGING FOR VICTORY

'I did not know my loss
Till one day twelve months later suddenly
I leaned upon my spade.'

                    (Edward Thomas)

We always knew it would be hard
    To uproot the concrete patio
The previous occupants had laid
    In our suburban, sun-lit yard,
To dig up nearly two decades
    Of stone and let the garden grow.

It took three broken spades, two picks,
    And several blistered pairs of hands
Before we knew we were in trouble;
    Four full skips of broken bricks
And we were still knee-deep in rubble,
    Ruin, broken flags and sand,

Still trying to dig through what remained
    Of some house knocked down long ago,
Whose ruined walls and shattered glass,
    Cracked tiles and bricks and slates contained
The history we'd to shift for grass
    To repossess this yard and grow.

Such archaeology was more
    Than blistered hands unused to toil
Had bargained for, so we applied
    Some garden-centre-bagged manure
And added bits of dirt and tried
    To tell the grass that it was soil.

And what we grew, of course, was not
　　A green and pleasant English lawn
But greying, wispy weeds instead,
　　A balding patch, a wretched plot
Of disappointed grass, half-dead,
　　A barren, blasted garden, *thrawn*.

The politics of laying turf
　　Lie just beneath our muddy boots,
Where roots go deep or not at all
　　And anything of any worth
Grows down as deep as it grows tall,
　　And nothing grows that has no roots.

Yet something lovely still survives
　　Where lumpen weeds uncurl their green
Utopias on tendrils growing
　　Through the bin-bags in the drive,
Their blazing flag-red flowers showing
　　What this garden could have been.

THE BEASTS OF ENGLAND

The long, long night is o'er at last,
   The beastly tyrant slain,
The light of dawn breaks in the east
   Saluting Freedom's reign!

Though cowards flinch and traitors sneer,
   The last fight's faced and won,
The age of Cant is past at last,
   The age of Truth begun.

For Manor Farm is free again,
   And Farmer Jones restored,
And upstart porkers everywhere
   Have had their bacon cured.

Their nasty brutish, short-lived rule
   Is finally o'erthrown,
And market day in Willingdon
   The drinks are all on Jones.

Arise, arise, and hark ye
   To the news from Manor Farm,
Where beasts are free to roam again
   And England's safe from harm,

Where Nature's just a fable for
   The swinish multitude,
Where some are meant to eat a lot
   But most are meant for food,

Where History can be boiled down
   To just a lump of lard,
And every good idea ends up
   In Alfred Simmond's yard.

But things look bad on Manor Farm,
　　And Jones is overdrawn,
The sheep are in the meadow
　　And the cows are in the corn,

And the harvest fields are full of weeds,
　　And overrun by rats,
And the windmill doesn't work these days
　　And the dairy's full of cats,

And in the ruined harvest poppies
　　Nod their sleepy heads,
And the sheep and goats are all mixed up,
　　And the geese and ducks are dead,

For Jones employs three foxes called
　　Dominion, Rank and Greed,
Who guard the hen-house door at night
　　For more than chicken-feed.

From Foxwood Farm to Pinchfield Farm
　　The masters celebrate
The liberated superpower
　　That's now a Third World State,

And toast the Red Lion taproom hero,
　　Now turned auctioneer,
Who's selling off his meadows
　　Just to keep himself in beer.

And sharp-eyed neighbours shake their heads
　　And say it's for the best –
It's better to die hungry than
　　To eat but be oppressed.

If Manor Farm goes to the dogs
    The reason's plain to see:
The stupid brutes who thought to choose
    To eat but not be free.

So raise the scarlet standard high,
    In every market place,
French fries and coke and burgers shall
    Unite the human race,

Arise ye starvelings, kneel no more,
    Your dreams have come to pass,
You poor and hungry multitudes
    Shall eat your fill of grass.

LETTER TO RANDALL SWINGLER

I thought I ought to drop you just a line
    To let you know your life at last is done –
By which I do not mean your life but mine,
    No, not *my life*, my *life of you*, the one
I've spent (my progress has been limacine
    I guess) what seems like a half a life-time on,
And which is why, though you may think it daft,
I'm pleased to say you've reached your final draft.

One death's enough for anyone, I know,
    And yours (which you supposed long overdue
Since the assault on Monte Camino)
    Outside that pub on Shaftesbury Avenue,
The hardening artery of old Soho,
    A stone's throw from the Party's old HQ,
Cannot (at fifty-eight) have been much fun –
But I can't resurrect you till you're done!

Of course, you did not ask to be exhumed,
    You probably think the whole thing's quite absurd;
I don't suppose you like being disentombed,
    Or waking up to find you're disinterred;
I'm sorry, also, if I have presumed
    Upon our friendship, but from what I've heard
I hope you will not think me too familiar
(I'd hate to be accused of necrophilia).

I know so much about you now I feel
    I know you better than I know myself;
Your years of anger, wartime love's ordeal,
    Your wild affairs, despairs and broken health,
Your disappointed English commonweal
    Remaindered like your books upon my shelf,
The only place it can be really said
We co-exist – because we're never read.

14

There's stuff in here I wish I'd never seen –
    The failed ideals and failing hopes that start
To take on flesh beneath my spade, between
    The empty bottles and the failing heart,
This lock of long-dead hair from Geraldine,
    The sense of failure you made into art.
But if I'm going to dig you up the price is
Playing sexton to your many faults and vices.

I want your help, you see, I need to learn
    The way you faced a lifetime of defeat
Without despair, the way you learned to turn
    Dismay and doubt into a world complete,
The knack you had of knowing when to burn
    Your bridges without sounding the retreat.
I need you at this century's sorry end,
And not just as my subject, as my friend.

But we've not yet been properly introduced.
    Although you're dead, I feel I should explain
Just why this clumsy stranger's come to roost
    Among the memorabilia in your brain.
It's dark in here, but now I'm getting used
    To following the thread through your demesne,
Deciphering the desperate, antique scrawls
You left unsigned upon the blood-stained walls.

By time and place and class and education
    We couldn't be more different if we'd tried,
Estranged by war and age and generation
    (I was still in the Juniors when you died),
But with or without your co-operation,
    Within my life of you, our worlds collide
(I have just given you a heart-attack,
While listening to an early Velvet's track!).

15

The world has changed a bit since you last died,
    As you'll find out, we're in a proper state;
So you will have to trust me as your guide
    To planet Earth in 1998
Where hunger, homelessness and genocide
    Are really back in fashion, Randall mate,
And reason's overthrown and human hopes
Rest now in shopping, prayers and horoscopes.

I wish that I could say we had progressed,
    But to be honest things are looking dire,
We've fucked up on a scale you never guessed
    (See chapter 24, *passim*, Isaiah),
Enough to make the long dead dead depressed,
    And half the living look for some Messiah
To land its flying saucer and absolve us
(The other half are cleaning their revolvers).

I'll do my best to bring you up-to-date:
    Dag Hammerskjold *was* murdered after all,
The Soviets fucked it up in '68,
    The US lost in Vietnam, the Wall
Came down, Mandela's now the head of state,
    And One Sixth of the World has since the Fall
Been sold by Russian democrats on tanks
To gangsters, junkies, priests and merchant banks.

This island's meanwhile ruled by earnest swots
    From public schools who call themselves New Labour
(Somehow they make the old lot look like Trots!)
    Who while exhorting us to love our neighbours
Spend half their time engaged in palace-plots
    Or rattling their wallets and their sabres.
It's sometimes hard to say which is obscener,
Their taste for air-strikes or their smug demeanour.

Of what you called the Left, we're on the ropes,
    We're finished, stuffed, knocked out, and there alas is
No point at all in getting up your hopes
    About the old industrial working-classes –
They don't exist, except in TV soaps;
    The world wants Golden Calves, not Golden Asses!
The Party's over now, not just in crisis,
And there's no sign of any help from Isis.

And you thought things were bad in '56!
    These last ten years I've watched that good old cause
Replaced by what they call post-politics,
    Where post-colonial empires start new wars,
Post-fascists burn post-immigrants for kicks,
    And post-diluvian economic laws
Post-date the cheques for things we thought we owned –
And yes, the revolution's been post-poned.

And now, of course, it suddenly transpires
    The Soviets never were a threat at all!
The only threat to Freedom were the liars
    Who said they were to keep us all in thrall
With hell-fire sermons threatening to fry us.
    Their lies unravel like that magic ball
Of Theseus until the winding threads
Reveal the monsters sleeping in our heads.

There's other things you need to know, e.g.
    That Crossman never made it all the way,
That Orwell narked for Mayhew's IRD,
    Encounter was run by the CIA,
And Stalin (we know now) was KGB
    While Dylan was a drunk, and Ben was gay.
Each week the revelations get more silly
Like Claud's 'Small Earthquake – No-one Hurt – in Chile'.

The poetry scene you'll find's full of surprises,
    It's popular (or so we like to claim),
And London's now awash with bloody prizes,
    And poets these days have to make their name
In sassy, smart, ironical disguises
    (And yet somehow so many sound the same).
Accountants celebrate the verse revival
While poetry mags still struggle for survival.

These days Old Grigson's bite has lost its savour,
    And Eliot's reputation's been revised,
And Cecil's down but Louis's back in favour,
    And Laurie Lee has just been televised,
While Dylan's now regarded as a raver,
    And bloody Orwell has been canonised.
Though critics' blessings come and go the news is
Somehow still bad for those blessed by the Muses.

You hated fuss, the tiresome ballyhoo
    They call success, the clamorous world's applause,
You'd laugh at this, I guess (a life of *you*!),
    And maybe some lives don't require encores
(I think I'd want to skip the replay too
    If my life turned out half as hard as yours).
But you don't need to fear the bitch success,
Because, you see, your life's still in a mess...

Biography's an art that simplifies
    (A *life* in just a 100k words!)
But though I've tried to cut you down to size
    (You are already slimmer by a third)
It can't be done, as now I realise;
    To write a life of you's simply absurd.
I've done my best to fit you on the page,
But I can't make you fit this narrow age.

18

'We don't do minor poets,' they explain,
    If you're neglected, you're a minor figure,
So minor poets like you should not complain
    If you're forgot while 'major' poets get bigger.
You ought to see the door-stop lives that strain
    Our bookshelves with their documentary rigour,
Of those who, when alive were barely read,
Have somehow put on weight now they are dead.

These bloody great breeze-block biographies
    Are massive as the lives they hold are slender
(You can imagine just how many trees
    Will die to make the life of Stephen Spender!)
As though by being big they'll somehow squeeze
    A space on shelf, review page and agenda.
Three portly Cyril Connolly's a scandal
When there's no room for even one slim Randall.

The rule is certain weightless poets survive
    While others sink as though they're set in lead;
They did not want you when you were alive
    And want you even less now you are dead,
And every publisher (now twenty-five)
    To whom I've sent you's sent you back and said
That though they like you they can't sell a word
Of poets of whom the public has not heard.

But that is why I wrote the bleeding book!
    And since most every word you ever wrote
Is out of print then we are out of luck;
    It looks as though my campaign to promote
Your verse is knacked, old son, we've come unstuck,
    The chance that they will publish you's remote.
It's clear that even though you're in your box,
They still think you are dead unorthodox.

You know, I thought the buggers would have bitten
    At least the wild Fitzrovian drinking scenes,
If not the stuff you wrote with Auden/Britten,
    Those wartime CEMA tours of Geraldine's,
Your opera for the Festival of Britain,
    The witchunt at the Beeb, your magazines –
Although I'm not surprised, it makes me furious
To know our literary culture's so incurious.

You should have gone to China or to Spain,
    Been photographed in Berlin, young and tanned,
And clenched your fists in Hyde Park in the rain,
    Sung Russian songs you didn't understand,
Then ripped your Party card up to complain
    When History turned out not the way you planned,
And made your fortune as a renegade
Because your Revolution was betrayed.

Instead you heard in England's changing seasons
    A song beneath the bitter wind's lament:
That though the Autumn rains on human reason
    And Summer's bright inheritance is spent,
Though rebel Spring has buried its green treason
    Beneath the soil of England's discontent,
The English commons shall be unenclosed
When Winter's long imperial rule's deposed.

We like our Thirties poets to make us smile,
    To prove idealists are all charlatans,
When to be young meant writing infantile
    Verse plays for horny-handed Calibans,
Reporting on those jolly Moscow Trials,
    Declaiming odes to Soviet Five Year Plans;
You should have penned more solemn Russophilia
Which we'd forgive as prep-school juvenilia.

In war we like our poets unafraid
    To die unknown, unpublished, in their primes,
Or join the MOI and get well paid
    For writing propaganda pantomimes.
You know, you really could have had it made
    If you'd just put the blame on 'tragic times'.
But five years overseas with the Eighth Army –
No wonder Bush House war poets thought you barmy!

At least you should have taken a commission,
    And not that single stripe at Anzio,
You may have been a poet and musician
    But honestly – a humble NCO!
You put us in a difficult position,
    Despite your medal we don't want to know.
The booktrade's like the Army, more or less,
And they don't want Lance-Corporals in the mess!

We don't, you see, like heroes any more
    (Except in sport) and Duty just seems quaint;
And no-one gives a toss about your War;
    We're nervous in the presence of a saint;
Utopian dreamers simply make us snore,
    So you and I've not much cause for complaint
If in the car-boot sale of our desires
Grand Narratives like ours cannot find buyers.

You chased the minotaur up from Salerno
    To victory in 1945,
You faced it on the banks of the Volturno,
    And though a part of you did not survive,
Emerging from the heart of the inferno
    You showed us what it means to be alive,
And how we cannot find the labyrinth's gate
Unless we face the monsters we create.

But having killed the monster you returned
   Beneath the blackened, perjured sails of peace
To find that what you hoped the world had learned
   Had been already sacrificed in Greece,
To know the world you thought that you had earned
   Was ransomed to appease the horned beast.
And poor Europa was again deceived
And war's next generations were conceived.

And we have lived for almost five decades
   Within the shadow chill of your defeat,
Afraid to live beneath the sun, afraid
   To leave our Winter's cave in case we meet
Our monster selves and know we've been betrayed
   By fire-lit tales of humans who would eat
Us lost in labyrinth dreams of cave-dark night,
Afraid to stand erect beneath the light.

I've spent too long inside this catacomb,
   The memories here seem mine as much as yours –
The shadows in the dormitory gloom
   Familiar as the painted minotaurs
Who guard the narrow entrance to your tomb
   Behind these unmarked, locked and shell-pocked doors.
And there your life and work must stay unread
Until the day the sea gives up its dead.

So this will have to do for now, old friend,
   I'm sorry I've disturbed you for so long,
Although I've tried, I cannot still pretend
   There's any point in trying to prolong
Your life, you're doubly dead! So let me send
   You back beneath the earth where you belong,
The never-finished manuscript that says
That death's the only exit from this maze.

THE MASK OF FREEDOM

I slept beside the river Tees
    And dreamed we'd lost our liberties,
That blindfold Justice was in chains,
    And tyrants ruled the world again.

But when I woke I heard the cheers
    Of Freedom ringing in my ears,
The forty-year-long Cold War won,
    The reign of Peace at last begun.

So I arose and went to greet
    The dancing crowds upon the street,
Saluting Freedom's victory
    And singing songs of Liberty.

And I met Freedom on the way.
    She wore a mask like Pinochet.
I drank with Freedom in the bar
    And drank a toast to Salazar.

We met again around the block
    And talked for hours of Papa Doc.
I saw her in a limousine
    Driving round the Philippines.

I heard her knocking on the door
    Before she left for East Timor.
The next day on the way to work
    We shared a taxi with de Klerk.

I put her on the mantelpiece
    Beside Bolivia and Greece.
I later met her down the lane
    On holiday in Franco's Spain.

And I saw Freedom wreathed in smiles
   Rejoicing on the Falkland Isles,
I watched her walking, dressed in black,
   On the road back from Iraq.

And Freedom came into my parlour
   Home on leave from Guatemala,
Home from Mozambique, Korea,
   Angola, Laos, Kampuchea,

El Salvador, Afghanistan,
   Honduras, Panama, Iran,
Namibia, Cuba, Cyprus, Ghana,
   Nicaragua, Guyana,

Vietnam and Indonesia,
   Belgian Congo, White Rhodesia,
Paraguay, the Argentine,
   Sudan, Grenada, Palestine,

And all the dirty little wars
   That Freedom's waged behind closed doors.
For only in the last resort,
   With Downing Street in full support,

Does Freedom send in her marines
   In full view of our TV screens.
She much prefers a little coup,
   Where blindfold Justice can't pursue:

The letterbombs so freely sent,
   The expertise so kindly lent
To death squads, hit squads, torture squads,
   The landmines, napalm, cattleprods,

24

Supplied to tinpot Third World juntas,
   The bounty paid to Dyak hunters
Hunting down the Chinese Reds
   And bringing back their severed heads.

The dollars with which Freedom buys
   Agents provocateurs and spies,
The free trade-unions in the pay
   Of Pentagon and CIA,

The flight of money, export freeze,
   The trade embargo, credit squeeze,
Returning exiles on the border,
   Bringing with them law and order,

The tanks surrounding Parliament,
   The bullets for the President,
The rigged elections, Te Deums,
   The bodies in the stadiums,

The cash and coke exchanged for arms,
   The peasants who have lost their farms,
The children who have lost their mothers,
   Fathers who have lost their brothers,

Union leaders, workers, singers,
   The artists who have lost their fingers,
The bodies of the disappeared
   In coups that Freedom's engineered,

In all the dirty little wars
   The Free World fought in Freedom's cause,
And all the dirty, blood-stained tricks
   Of CIA and MI6

That kept the Free World safe and free
    From comic-commie tyranny.
And Freedom took me by the hand
    And said she hoped I'd understand,

That if her champions disregard
    The rule of law in her backyard,
Or if they've taken liberties
    While fighting Freedom's enemies,

She's sorry if they're mine or yours,
    But they were taken in good cause.
About those lies from Vietnam,
    She said she did not give a damn

For Freedom's champions in the West
    Must guard our Freedoms while we rest
So we can slumber in our beds
    Untroubled by those nightmare Reds,

Those enemies of Liberty
    Who did not want to be set free,
Who thought it just an empty phrase
    Behind which tyrants hide their ways,

Who never stood a bloody chance,
    Who watched her bloody tide advance,
Who saw their every hope retreat
    From disappointment to defeat,

Those hopeless Reds whose hopes beside
    Her many triumphs were so few,
Who were no match for genocide,
    Who fell to earth like morning dew.

DURKIN'S CAMP, 1948

From Newport, Saltersgill and Brambles Farm
The homeless squatters filled the army camps
And led by Reds just out of uniform,
Defied police and council, freezing damp
And a People's Government so quick to shore
Up private property but slow to build
For those who'd fought and won the People's War
But found the People's Peace still unfulfilled.

And when the PLA, a few months later,
Approached the Yellow River, lives were lost
And Teesside Reds discovered that they'd crossed
From last year's heroes into Cold War traitors,
Their homeless hopes now camped like refugees
Along the freezing Yangtze and the Tees.

HELL, UTOPIA AND MIDDLESBROUGH

'It is deserted, shops are boarded up, many houses windowless, many lots vacant, dust whirls in the wind past the unpainted house-front: it looks as if a plague has visited it. This is not the effect of depression, or of war and bombs... the awful warning of depopulated St Hilda's... is a prototype from which city plan-ners of the present and future can learn a great deal.' (John Piper, 1945)

Our circulation really needs attention,
    Our car-park balance suffers from fatigue,
Our urban form is far too poor to mention,
    Our shops are just not in the premier league;
Investment levels, frankly, are a worry,
    The office market's verging on collapse,
Our confidence won't come back in a hurry,
    And our industry's been sold off to the Japs;
Our retail centre's in the wrong location,
    Our night-time leisure offer needs expanding,
Our cultural life requires co-ordination,
    Our entertainments profile needs rebranding.
It might come as a shock to you and me –
    But we're not as attractive as we thought,
We ain't as vibrant as we used to be,
    And not half so dynamic as we ought.
How hard it is to satisfy the planners!
    This side of hell, a long way from utopia,
We march beneath the splendid, ragged banners
    Of shoestring dreams that just keep getting ropier.
In scruffy towns like this we join together
    To find (says Aristotle) what we want:
A place to sleep protected from the weather,
    Untroubled by that moonlight on Vermont,
Where though at night we hear the outcast calls
    Beyond the pale, within the tangled wood,
The morning sees us climb the city walls
    To know what makes life civilised and good.

In Middlesbrough, utopia or hell
    Such aspirations plot their downward curve;
Among the dreary plains of Asphodel
    We get the shabby towns that we deserve.
Somehow the best-laid plans, e.g. Max Lock's,
    That grid-iron model North Square in St Hilda's,
 Don't work out as they should; the future mocks
    The shiny, bright intentions of the builders.
The story of the brave new town of Pease
    Must make all planners everywhere feel glum –
The tale of how Utopia-on-Tees
    Within two decades turned into a slum.
And yet there's also something reassuring
    About the way towns don't grow as they're planned:
Utopia can sometimes seem, well, boring
    To those who like the failed and second-hand.
The thought of brave-new-worlds provokes a yawn
    In sleepy citizens who want instead
A town that's slightly crumpled and well worn,
    The future like a still-warm, unmade bed.
What most of us like best is what we know
    And what we know is somewhere in between
The sum of what we've paid and what we owe:
    The people, and the towns, we could have been.
Beneath these streets lie other streets, like maps
    Of better towns than this, and better lives,
Where still the memory of what perhaps
    We all might one day be somehow survives.

COINING IT

When work brought workless working men to build
This town, they melted down their speech to make
A home-grown, home-sick coinage, semi-skilled,
But rough and ready made for answering back;
A common currency with which to trade
In hungry memories of County Clare
And Welsh and Cornish pits for work which paid
In kind and made a home of anywhere.

Now workless working men leave home again
To work in Saudi, Norway and Australia,
Well paid for all the longing years they'll spend
Away from home in accents stamped with failure,
And cash the common rhythms of the Tees
For unfamiliar foreign currencies.

SONG

Look, I'm sorry if this sounds unduly bitter,
I don't want to seem cynical or grim,
But when my time is up and I've drained life's loving cup,
You can use this for my crematory hymn:

    Don't be disconcerted when you're knackered,
    And don't look so crestfallen when you're beat,
    It's bound to get a lot worse yet,
    And there's no point being upset,
    So you'd better get accustomed to defeat.

And there's nothing you can do to make things better,
No matter how you try, things just get worse,
So when all is said and done, and I've had my bit of fun,
I hope they'll use this for my headstone verse:

    Don't be surprised when you're outwitted,
    Don't be dismayed when you're denied,
    There's more disasters still to come,
    And there is no point looking glum,
    Cos you'll always end up on the losing side.

When things look bad there's still more room for failure,
The last defeat's the prelude to the next,
The strong will always beat the weak, and we're on a
   losing streak,
So feel free to use this for my funeral text:

    Being right just isn't part of the equation,
    It's not much help to you when you go bust,
    Cos History is perverse,
    And like Midas in reverse,
    Each golden chance we have we turn to dust.

For God's sake never think you're on a winner,
Don't fool yourself, you're going to lose again,
So when I've pulled the final straw, and I'm lying at death's
   door,
I hope I'll croak my last to this refrain:

> Bad times to want a Revolution,
> Bad times to call yourself a Red:
> When everything you do
> Leaves you feeling just as blue
> At least you can't feel much worse when you're dead.

MARXISM AND SMOKING

'Capital will not even pay for the cigars I smoked writing it.'
(Marx to Paul Lafargue)

So many times, Fidel and me,
   We've tried to give up smoking,
Two weeks today I smoked my last –
   My last? You must be joking!

That's it, I said, my lungs are sore,
   I'm running short of breath,
I love this lovely world too much
   To want to hurry death.

What's more, tobacco's just a scam,
   A multinational racket,
Exploiting human weakness to
   Make some fat cat a packet.

How did I ever start this lark?
   Why am I so weak-willed?
To think of all the smoke-filled rooms,
   The ashtrays I have filled's

Enough to make we choke with guilt,
   Unqualified remorse,
To make me want to start to stop
   Again. And yet of course

Just two weeks on the other side,
   Two weeks since my last drag,
There's nothing I want more just now
   Than one more one last fag!

The fight continues, as it were,
    In deals I cut between
Rewards and punishments with fingers
    Stained with nicotine.

The best intentions, every one,
    Go up in smoke one day,
And nothing's left but ash and dust
    And death is on the way.

The history of smoking's full
    Of broken resolutions,
Just like, in fact, the strange museum
    Of broken revolutions,

Where courage, hubris, weakness, guilt,
    Are laid out as exhibits,
A spectre haunting Europe with
    An anti-social habit:

The cigarette case Lenin used's
    Now in a mausoleum,
As proof that even giants have lungs
    Of clay if we could see 'em;

And here's the weird device they used
    When Brezhnev was in power,
To clamp his mouth with wire to keep
    Him down to one an hour;

And that's the pipe that once was gripped
    Beneath that grim moustache
While signing grim decrees that turned
    The world's one hope to ash.

While Marx thought smoking gave him boils,
  Bakunin liked to choke
On fifty fat cigars a day
  And Trotsksy didn't smoke,

So smoking Bolsheviks were asked
  In Smolny's teeming halls
To nip out for a fag break through
  A hole cut in the wall.

And Harry Pollitt smoked cigars
  To ape the ruling classes,
To prove that nothing but the best
  Was fit to give the masses,

And Johnny Gollan once rolled up
  With Ho Ho Ho Chi Minh
Who showed us how to stub out evil
  Empires in the bin.

Down smoky Congress corridors
  And dusty District meetings
The wheezing ghosts of coughing Reds
  Light up, a self-defeating

Cancer ward of loss and pain
  And misspent lives and waste,
The fag end of a politics,
  The morning-after taste

Of one too many cigarettes
  And not enough good answers.
The rimming ashtrays mark the years
  Until they total cancer,

And all that's solid melts into
    The air till we must deal
With who and what and where we are
    And face at last the real

Material facts of our existence –
    Love, work, struggle, death –
Which every smoker knows who hears
    The rasping on their breath.

But if the best intentions must
    Go up in smoke one day,
If nothing's left but ash and dust
    And death is on the way –

Get stuck in now, smoke all you want,
    Breathe deeply till you canna,
And don't forget the very best
    Tobacco's from Havana!

Red smokers of the world unite!
    We'll beat the bastards yet,
This lovely world's to be enjoyed,
    Just like a cigarette.

Between necessity, desire
    And need's a politics
That's understood by all who ever
    Cadged a Number 6.

What makes all revolutions start's
    A kind of death-defying
Promethean disobedience
    To live until you're dying.

CURTAINS

While plotters plotted, faxes faxed,
And tanks rolled into Moscow town,
The curtains in the common room
Kept falling down, falling down.

AFTER VIRGIL

My luck's to follow unambitious household gods
While others have to run from ethnic-cleansing squads,

To live so far from History's bloody storyline,
Where no-one's going to try to murder me and mine.

We breakfast to the sound of shells on Radio Four,
Although our kitchen has not yet been hit, and war,

Like History, happens somewhere else, a world away,
A world with just enough atrocities each day

To fill the morning's *Guardian* with atrocious news.
While others have to fight in wars they did not choose

My luck's to live in such a quiet place and age,
To doodle in the margins of the century's page.

While others kill for hatred, fear, survival, power,
We have to be at work in less than half an hour.

We do not need to fear the anger of the poor,
The lines of hungry refugees outside the door.

My luck's to be alive in such a peaceful age,
To listen every morning in a helpless rage

Between the Money News and What the Papers Say,
The baying back-bench jingo chorus on *Today*,

As accusations of civilian deaths are traded
And in the bloody process something is degraded.

TALE FROM OVID

You might be handsome, true or smart,
   Or pretty, wise and plucky,
Good at sport and games or art,
   Or talented and lucky,

But every mortal ends up dead,
   The gods have fixed the odds,
So if you want to die in bed
   Don't fuck around with gods.

For wealth's a turn-on, so they say,
   And when they're in the mood
The powerful get their end away,
   The rest of us get screwed.

From sun-burnt Semele till now
   The world's been run by ogres,
Who like old Zeus just don't know how
   To keep it in their togas.

While those who live on heaven's summit
   Like a bit of clay,
Olympians who like to slum it
   Don't expect to pay.

Like daytime soaps and royalty,
   Your average randy god
Shows mortals little loyalty
   Once he has shot his wad,

And turns the woman he's just laid
   Into a tree or flower,
To show the world that she's just paid
   The price of fucking power.

Don't listen to their lies, my friend,
    Their promises and tricks,
For if you do you know you'll end
    Up face down in the Styx,

Or torn apart by hunting packs
    Of TV journalists,
Pursued around the world by fax,
    And stone-eyed columnists.

For even gods must make excuses
    (Hera's *such* a bitch),
The moral if you mess with Zeus is:
    Don't fuck with the rich.

So let's enjoy it, while we can,
    Allow a little chortle,
As through the heavens falls a man
    Who thought he was immortal,

Who thought he only had to smile
    And look a bit sincere
And hang around with Ares while
    He wiped away a tear,

Who almost lost his god-like crown,
    Turned by his misdemeanours
Into a spunk stain on a gown
    And taken to the cleaners.

An image of the age perhaps,
    To end this Age of Brass,
When no more would-be godlike chaps
    Shall fuck the working-class,

And whether you are true or smart,
    Or pretty, wise and plucky,
Good at sport and games or art,
    Or talented and lucky,

We will no longer watch the skies
    Or fear the patterned stars,
But see the world through mortal eyes
    And know at last it's ours.

CRASH! BANG! WALLOP!

Crash! Bang! Wallop!
Amazing news!
It's not just the Reds
And the foreigners and Jews
Who need to watch out
Because (wouldn't you know it?)
Jean Marie le Pen
Hates modern poets!

> As well as people
> Who come from Algiers,
> Jean Marie le Pen
> Hates onomatopoeias.

You'd think that the boys
At FN HQ
Would have rather more
Important things to do,
Like whipping up hatred,
Whipping up fear,
To bother with the harmless
Onomatopoeia.

> But honest, it's true
> From what I hear
> Jean Marie le Pen
> Hates onomatopoeias.

When they hear the word culture
They reach for their blue pens,
Cos they don't like noise
In le Pen's FN,
For Postmodern Fascists
There's not much worse
Than onomatopoeia
In contemporary verse.

It may sound daft
But it appears
That Jean Marie le Pen
Hates onomatopoeias.

Crash! Bang! Wallop!
The patriots are here,
A brick through your window
Wrapped in onomatopoeia.
These fun-loving guys
Are not averse to violence,
But they prefer reading
Verse in silence.

He may be bonkers
But it's true I fear
That Jean Marie le Pen
Hates onomatopoeias.

With an Eech! and an Ouch!
And a bit of a Crunch!
You can't ignore
This crazy bunch.
They don't like me
And they don't like you,
Not liking things
Is what they do.

I know that it sounds
A little bit queer,
But Jean Marie le Pen
Hates onomatopoeias.

With a Tick, Tock, Tick,
And a Tock, Tick, Tock,
The National Front
Put back the clock,
Harassing words
That they don't like,
Just like in the days
Of the old Third Reich.

So tell everybody
Loud and clear
That Jean Marie le Pen
Hates onomatopoeia.

Bang! on your desks
And Clap! your hands,
Make a lot of noise
Before it's banned,
Clomp! your feet
And Thump! that table,
Blow them a raspberry
While you're still able.

It's so hard to believe
(But he seems sincere)
That Jean Marie le Pen
Hates onomatopoeias.

But don't ever forget
Before it ends in tears,
We've rather more to lose
Than our onomatopoeias;
If le Pen could do
What he really wants to do,
It's not just poets
Who would go Boo Hoo.

ONCE BITTEN

What happens when the usual tricks
  Don't work as once they did –
The silver bullets, crucifix,
  The nailed-down coffin lid?

When running water's lost its power
  To make a Dracul run,
And holy wafers, garlic flowers
  All wither in the sun?

When nothing tickles the Undead
  Like driven, pointy stakes,
And vampires never lose their heads
  And morning never breaks?

When History's an old re-run
  Of hammy, Hammer-horrors,
And Dracula admires his tan
  Reflected in the mirror?

The old traditions make us smile,
  But parasites don't die,
Though monsters sometimes change their style,
  Still they bleed us dry,

And frightened peasants in the inn
  Recount new bedtime stories
Of a man with a terrible vampire grin
  More chilling than the Tories.

Count Alucard's abroad once more
  And looking for your vote,
But if you're ill or weak or poor
  You'll get it in the throat.

New suits and ties cannot disguise
　　These bloodless life-blood suckers,
For all they try to modernise
　　They're still repulsive fuckers.

The grave is bare, they're back again,
　　It's no use us pretending,
When vampires claim to feel your pain
　　You know the bleeding ending.

ONE WRITING AGAINST HIS MEMBER

'the warmth of her body pervading to mine, the bed now warm
with our heat, her lying on top of me, her breasts heavy to my
chest, the heat of her womanhood seating my scrotum, my lying
there without love, without hope, limp, defeated...'
(Stuart Bell, Paris Sixty-Nine)

To every man there comes the day
   When facts can't be denied,
A nil response from what was once
   A source of strength and pride.

It's just a way that Nature has
   To gently let you know
You're past your prime and that it's time
   To pack your bags and go.

What's gone is gone and won't come back,
   You can't disguise the truth,
A wilting cock is like a clock
   That marks your passing youth.

The very thought of surgery
   Just makes my member shrink,
And magic pills can't stiffen quills
   Once they've run out of ink.

It's only natural after all,
   You've had your hour of glory,
A little lapse is just perhaps
   A small *momento mori.*

But in your case it's been so long
   I really can't remember
Just how it felt below the belt
   To have a proper member.

There's no escaping from the flesh,
    It leaves you in no doubt,
Let's face it son, you've had your fun,
    Your membership's run out.

You're not the man you were, old cock,
    You can't maintain the pace,
You've failed the test, you're past your best,
    You're just a waste of space,

You're like a dog without a bone,
    A mast without a keel,
A wilting rose, a punctured hose,
    A bell without a peal,

A French stick left out in the rain,
    A novel no-one's read,
A ziggurat that's fallen flat,
    A pencil with no lead,

A falling tower, a leaning spire,
    A lamp without a wick,
A pointless flop who's for the chop,
    A useless little prick.

But don't look glum, things might look up,
    You're not yet on the shelf,
And to be frank, a merchant bank
    Might help you feel yourself.

And though, of course, I'll not forget
    The moments we enjoyed,
For old time's sake it's time to shake
    Hands with the unemployed.

REPLAY

Though we come from a town
Where we haven't any money
And it always rains
And it's never very sunny,
Yet we manage to escape
Just once a year
To drown our sorrows
In Wembley beer,
To London town
Where the streets are made of money
And it never ever rains
And it's always very sunny.
And whether we win
Or whether we lose,
The London press
Knows what to do,
Sunning themselves
By the banks of the Thames,
Sun-dried commentators
Reach for their pens
To write about a town
Where we haven't any money
And it always rains
And it's never very sunny…

METHUSELAH'S LOSERS

A quick one-two, a turn, a screaming shot,
    Back off the post, a run through the defence
To knock it straight back in, and though we've not
    Yet touched the ball, we're one-nil down against
A team whose youth and energy subdues us
And makes us feel a bunch of hopeless losers.

Because Methuselah's too long to go
    On Third Division league and fixture lists
We play as Losers and/or Meths – as though
    We only lose because we're always pissed!
There's better teams than us made up of boozers,
And being sober's no help to the Losers.

At least we are consistent; losing streaks
    Like ours take years and years of bloody training,
It's hard to be this bad, you need technique;
    So please don't get me wrong, we're not complaining,
We don't think being useless helps excuse us,
It's just that practice makes us perfect losers!

You do not have to win to feel the buzz
    Of sweat, testosterone and self-display;
Part circus show (including clowns like us),
    Part theatre, part athletics, part ballet,
A game designed for gents that's played by bruisers
Who are long past their prime (just like Meths Losers)

Who, stuck in check-out queues and traffic lights
    And meetings, still replay the games we've played
On Sunday mornings or on Wednesday nights,
    The well-timed tackles, passes, goals we've made,
The unrecorded triumphs which enthuse us
Enough to turn out weekly for the Losers.

I like defeat, its sweaty, human smell,
    Familiar as a much replayed own goal
Or spannered shot; this losing fits me well
    (Just like our too-tight strip!) and on the whole
I think a winning sequence would confuse us,
At least you know just where you are with losers.

While those who can afford it cheer success
    Via satellite TV and sponsors' boxes,
On sweaty 5-a-side courts we transgress
    The age's most unbending orthodoxies:
To be the worst! The thought somehow renews us:
Down with success! And up with all the losers!

Not coming first's an honourable aim
    When winning is the only Good; there's pride
In coming last, in losing every game,
    In being always on the losing side.
The games we really should have won accuse us:
Success belongs to others, not to losers.

Let's hear it then for those who're past their best;
    Without us there would not be many winners,
We're here to make the numbers up, the Rest,
    To teach the art of losing to beginners;
Their shiny, bright successes just amuse us,
For even winners have to play with losers.

So here's to hopeless losers everywhere
    Who know we're stuffed before we even start,
Who live with disappointment and despair,
    Who turn defeat into a kind of art;
An army of dissenters and refusers,
We'd change the world – if we weren't such good losers!

51

IN MEMORY OF MOGG WILLIAMS

Ten hours it took to get back home that night,
  The first eight hours by clumsy train
That stopped at every station on the way,
  An eight-hour shift through freezing rain
That turned to ice at Darlington, where our
  Much twocked old car'd been nicked again.

No problem finding what was left of it –
  Before I knew that it had been
Ripped off, someone had found it, said they knew
  The kids involved, but were not keen
To give their name (and who could blame them?) scared
  To testify to what they'd seen.

Two hours to wait on some windswept estate
  In freezing Darlo to be towed
Away; the radio pinched, the heater bust,
  And then round two a.m. it snowed!
Two hours to count the snowflakes as they fell
  Like broken glass across the road.

I wondered if you had this snow in Wales,
  And you up writing half the night
Black words that shone like coal through snow's blank page;
  Though morning melts the stuff we write
By night, there's still some art, like falls of snow,
  Can make the bleakest dawn seem bright.

How difficult it is to testify
  To what we think we know about
The freezing world beyond our own front doors
  When living seems to ladle out
Such numbing lumps of truth and beauty mixed
  With cold dismay and midnight doubt.

You testified to what you saw, all right,
    Up half the night inside your shed,
In books about the folk you lived among
    And not about the books you'd read,
Till pulling verse up by its bloody roots,
    You found them growing in your head.

Plain words and common speech was what you found,
    The poetry of common work,
A gift of tongues with which to testify
    And make that common history talk,
And more, a common faith that's strong enough
    To make the mountains rise and walk.

A common poet! A strange, uncommon sight
    In this poor land, where words are tied with strings
Of snobbery and class, and 'common' means
    Not what we share but just the things
That no-one cares to speak of in the cloistered
    Speech of courtiers and kings.

You were the real thing, Mogg old friend, a poet
    Who knew that every poet relies
On knowing whom they're talking to, that those
    Who don't soon end up talking lies
Or bollocks (just the kind Arts Councils like
    To publish and to subsidise!).

A laureate of smoky pubs and clubs,
    You never fell into the trap
Of getting drunk on words to make your verse
    Seem thirsty work to those whose snap
Reactions were the only ones you sought
    (If they don't like you, they won't clap!).

A miner and a major poet in one!
	You found a way to say what's true
In unironic, honest, common verse,
	Although the truth you spoke's taboo
To those who don't believe that art belongs
	To common, working folk like you.

Of course they wheel the usual reasons out –
	Poor spelling, Mogg, your tenses wrong,
Apostrophes misplaced, too earnest, *dull*,
	You should have known you'll not belong
So long as poetry's the property
	Of those who'd privatised the tongue.

'It's just incompetence, not rudeness,' Mogg;
	It never is, contempt's not planned,
It's not some kind of weird Arts Council plot
	To keep you out, your work's not *banned*,
It's just the lazy sound of closing doors
	On what they fear to understand.

But what you stood for, Mogg, will long survive
	The fashionable, the smart, the chic,
Will last until the world no longer needs
	The art of knowing how to speak
Not simply for, but with and to the anger
	Of the powerless and the weak.

You understood and sometimes shared the sense
	Of helpless, puzzled, common rage
Of those so fearful of tomorrow that
	They'd make a bloody Golden Age
Of hardship, hard work, dirt and poverty,
	And bitterness a living wage.

And yet that anger also leads towards
    The Golden City's shining streets,
A future I can't name for fear
    Of sounding flat as marching feet.
And though that future seems no nearer now,
    And though it's darkened by defeats,

And though we have to wait for night to pass,
    And watch the patient snow descend,
The dawn will hail the snow's republic, like
    An image of the day, old friend,
When all the world shall be revealed in common,
    Until we get there in the end.

THE HOUSE BEAUTIFUL

'from the place where he now stood, even to the end of the valley, the way was all along set so full of snares, traps, gins, and nets here, and so full of pits, pitfalls, deep holes, and shelving.' (John Bunyan)

From Houghton House the sleepy plain's
    A beer-mat scene of harvest gold,
Where citizens of sleep's domain
    Wake up to find their dreams gone cold
And England sold to profiteers
    In sleepy, sleepy Bedfordshire.

Between the quarries and the bricks
    Between the landfill and the clay,
All earthly aspiration sticks
    Hungover in the light of day,
Like those who sup on Bombadier
    In sleepy, sleepy Bedfordshire.

But something in this treeless vale
    Still stirs the yeast of earth-bound schemes,
Like prelate's broth and local ale
    And chiliastic sects that dream
Of Armageddon's panacea
    In sleepy, sleepy Bedfordshire.

Between the morning star and bed
    The valley sides are strange and steep
So pilgrims lay their sleepy heads
    As in a dream and yet not sleep
And see a vision shining clear
    In sleepy, sleepy Bedforshire.

He who would leave a tinker's cottage
    To prove some dreams are not for sale
Must learn to price a mess of pottage –
    (Twelve years banged up in Bedford gaol)
For peaceful dreams come very dear
    In sleepy, sleepy Bedfordshire,

As sleepy taxi drivers know who're called
   On midnight trips to even scores
In smack and cocaine border wars
   And end up dead to all the world;
Their progress marks the wild frontiers
   Of sleep in sleepy Bedfordshire.

And pilgrim tourists passing by
   Don't see the cracks between the streets,
They keep their eyes upon the sky
   And not the pit beneath their feet
Who follow steps that disappear
   Up wooden hills to Bedfordshire.

While Mansoul's fast asleep in bed
   The night takes flight on cobweb wings
And crawls inside the sleeper's head
   To lay the eggs of nightmare things
That breed the Diabolonian fears
   That stir in sleepy Bedfordshire.

But even sleepy English scenes
   Like this must choose to dream or wake
And know the difference between
   The two and waking help to make
The cold night's pitfalls disappear
   In sleepy, sleepy Bedfordshire.

What's lost by night's regained by day
   As morning washes Mansoul clean,
The sun comes up once more to slay
   The monsters of the night's ravine
And shows the sun-lit way shine clear
   On hills that lead from Bedfordshire.

JUST AS BLUE

A breezeless, sunny, Summer day
    At Brooke House Farm, and I'm just four
Or five, a town-mouse come to stay,
    Homesick perhaps, and not so sure
About this world that's fierce and strange
    And full of things from storybooks:
The giant oven in the range,
    The furnace doors I must not touch,

The home-made broom outside the door,
    The baking smells of gingerbread,
And everywhere the friendly, raw
    Tobacco smell of Uncle Fred;
The cellar with its froggy holes,
    A fox head stuffed with marble eyes,
The fences hung with rats and moles;
    The piglet wriggles in the sties,

The shippon gloom of dust and straw,
    The diesel stink of old machines,
The high-pitched smell of fresh manure,
    The dairy's chapel quiet, its clean
And polished, buttered, sunshine taste;
    The angry, barking dogs on chains
Whose unleashed fury must be faced
    If I'm to venture down the lane.

But here, against the haystack sides,
    A ladder climbs to heaven knows where,
A stair up which, half-terrified,
    I slither backwards into air,
Till halfway up the clouds unfold
    Their magic carpet in the skies,
A square of blue enframed with gold,
    A vast and roofless blue surprise.

58

How close the sky appears from here.
    No child could ever paint such blue
As this, an endless, hurting, clear
    And lovely, lonely, trespassed view.
Within this blue I've built a den,
    A musty house of bales of straw
To keep out stupid one-eyed hens,
    And hungry wolves outside the door.

How dreamy still and quiet it seems,
    As though the giant world is curled
Asleep and I'm inside a dream
    Of bean-stalks far above the world,
Where hay bales might be spun to gold,
    And happy endings are all true,
Where little pigs do not grow old,
    And skies are always just as blue.

As if I've had this dream before,
    Down tunnels made with itching legs
I reach to find, within the straw,
    A clutch of warm and feathered eggs,
Like magic beans which only grow
    When all the grown-ups are in bed,
Which lead to where all children know
    They grind your bones to make their bread.

The sleepy world below now stirs –
    The milking stalls' electric hum,
A distant tractor's muddy purrs,
    The background mumble of the glum
Suspicious cows, as they're pursued
    By Fe-fi-fo-ing dogs and men.
It's time to leave this solitude,
    The giant world's awake again.

AFTER ARAGON

'Parce que j'ai le coeur plein d'une autre defaite.'

1   *Lilacs and Roses*

O lovely months of blossom, months of magic,
    Cloudless May, and June that cut till it hurt,
I will never forget your lilacs and roses, the tragic
    Flowers that Spring hid beneath her skirts.

And I will never forget the crowds of Bank Holiday faces,
    The sunshine and the noisy queues, the carts with their loads
Of love, the presents from Belgium, the quarrels and embraces,
    The trembling air, the humming of bees on the roads,

The puzzled silence, the evenings peaceful and hazy,
    The roses beside the roads we travelled by,
And those who were stuck in tanks, surrounded by the crazy
    Crowds and the lilac scent, who were going to die.

I will never forget the wind of panic in the gardens,
    The soldiers who passed on the wings of fear in the breeze,
The frantic lines of traffic and the ironical guns,
    The pitiable luggage of the homeless refugees,

And a house in Normandy, on the edge of a wood at night,
    When all was quiet and even the enemy was asleep,
And we heard that Paris had fallen. I will never forget
    Those lilacs and roses, and the loves that we failed to keep.

I will never forget the fresh lilacs of Flanders,
    Flowers that sweetened the flesh of the young dead,
And you, the flowers of our retreat, the tender
    Roses, the colour of fire, distant and red.

My country's an abandoned wreck
    That rudderless has run aground,
And I'm the captain left on deck
    A shipwrecked king whose hopes are drowned,
Who rules only his grief.

To live is just to sit and wait,
    The wind can't help me when I weep,
And all I love I now must hate,
    What I have lost the world can keep.
I rule only my grief.

My heart may stop and beat no more,
    My blood may flow without its heat,
Now two and two do not make four
    For losers when they try to cheat.
I rule only my grief.

The sun may never rise again,
    The sky's the colour now of lead,
The Paris of my youth is gone,
    The flowers of the Spring are dead.
I rule only my grief.

Now all you birds can fly away
    And not come back for all I care,
I do not want your songs today,
    This is the kingdom of despair.
I rule only my grief.

As when they murdered Joan of Arc,
    These are the days of broken pride,
Both night and day the skies are dark,
    And France again is occupied,
I rule only my grief.

3   *Santa Espina*

I used to know a song that made
   My blood race and my pulse run fast,
And fire start like a heart in the grate,
   And I knew why the sky was blue at last.

A song that was caught on the edge of the breeze,
   Like a sob in the night, like the mermaids heard
In the salty revenge of the open seas,
   A song like the cry of migrating birds.

We whistled that song on sunless days,
   In unheroic, fallen times,
As a great people underground
   Saw tyrants perish in their dreams.

Its name was a garland of sacred thorns
   That crowned the forehead of God with blood,
A song that hammered flesh like a nail,
   Carving its wounds like a name cut in wood.

We hummed that tune since nobody dared
   To sing the song's forbidden words
But when the world was poxed with grief
   This song was our hope of being heard.

I listen today for that heart-rending air,
   But the world is too busy to know what it's lost,
The song sung by the murmuring streams
   As they run to the sea is now silenced by frost.

I listen in vain for the song of the thorn,
   But we who heard that old refrain
Have quite forgotten how it goes,
   And the singing woods are silent again.

I want to believe such music survives
    That those who are silenced will hear it and talk
And that one fine day the oppressed and the weak
    Will sing that song as they stand up and walk,

And I want to believe that the Son of Man,
    Will wear no more a crown of blood,
And we will sing at the tops of our voices
    And the hawthorn will flower and life will be good.

NOTES

p.11 'The Beasts of England' is the title of the anthem sung by the animals in George Orwell's *Animal Farm* (1945); the names in this poem are also taken from the novel.

p.14 Randall Swingler (1909–67) was an English lyric poet and a Communist; during the Second World War he fought with the Eighth Army in Italy, where he was awarded the Military Medal for bravery.

p.23 'The Mask of Freedom' is modelled loosely on Shelley's 'The Mask of Anarchy'.

p.28 'Hell, Utopia and Middlesbrough' is the title of a chapter in Thomas Sharp's *English Panorama* (1936); the oldest part of Middlesbrough is now known as St Hilda's; Max Lock led the Survey and Plan commissioned by Middlesbrough Council during the Second World War. This poem was originally commissioned for the launch of the Middlesbrough Town Centre Company, but was rejected on the grounds that potential investors in the town might not like it.

p.30 In 1872 Engels asked the General Council of the First International to ask the Middlesbrough branch 'whether it would be Irish or English'.

p.38 'After Virgil' draws on Cecil Day-Lewis's translation of *The Georgics of Virgil* (1943), Book II, lines 458–74, 493–512.

p.39 'Tale from Ovid' is based on a story which does not appear in Ted Hughes's translation of *Metamorphoses*.

p.47 'One Writing Against His Member' is an attempt to render into contemporary English Lord Rochester's 'One Writeing Against His Prick'; Stuart Bell is the Labour MP for Middlesbrough.

p.56 'The House Beautiful', where Christian stays in *The Pilgrim's Progress*, is based on Houghton House in Bedfordshire; 'Prelate's Broth' and a 'mess of pottage' were names given by English Puritans to the Anglican *Book of Common Prayer,* imposed on Dissenters after the Restoration; 'Mansoul' is the name given to Bedford in Bunyan's *The Holy War*, where the town is attacked by the (Royalist) 'Diabolonians'.

p.60 'Lilacs and Roses,' 'Richard II' and 'Santa Espina' are versions of poems by Louis Aragon written after the defeat of France in 1940 and published in *Le Crève-Coeur* (1942); 'Santa Espina' recalls the Sardana to which Catalan soldiers marched during the Spanish Civil War (and the theme song of Joris Ivens's film *Spanish Earth*).